COUNTDOWN TO SPACE

D0170549

FRIENDSHIP 7
First American in Orbit

Michael D. Cole

Series Advisor:
John E. McLeaish
Chief, Public Information Office, retired,
NASA Johnson Space Center

ENSLOW PUBLISHERS, INC.

44 Fadem Rd.   P.O. Box 38
Box 699   Aldershot
Springfield, N.J. 07081   Hants GU12 6BP
U.S.A.   U.K.

Library of Congress Cataloging-in-Publication Data

Cole, Michael D.
    Friendship 7: first American in orbit / Michael D. Cole.
        p. cm. — (Countdown to space)
    Includes bibliographical references and index.
    ISBN 0-89490-540-6
    1. Project Mercury (U.S.)—Juvenile literature. 2. Glenn, John, 1921– —Juvenile
literature. 3. Friendship 7 (Spacecraft)—Juvenile literature. 4. Glenn, John, 1921– .
[1. Project Mercury (U.S.) 2. Friendship 7 (Spacecraft)] I. Title. II. Title: Friendship
seven. III. Series.
TL789.8.U6M4537 1995
629.45′4— dc20   94-29433
                                                                           CIP
                                                                            AC

Printed in the U.S.A.

10 9 8 7 6 5 4 3 2 1   3 9082 06130955 8

Illustration Credits:
National Aeronautics and Space Administration (NASA), pp. 4, 6, 7, 9, 10,
11, 14, 15, 16, 18, 22, 24, 31, 33, 35, 36, 37, 38, 39, 40.

Cover Illustration:
National Aeronautics and Space Administration (NASA) (foreground);
© L. Manning/Westlight (background).

CONTENTS

John Glenn is helped into the Friendship 7 *spacecraft on the day of his history-making flight.*

Ready for Launch

"T minus one minute and counting. All systems are reported in Go condition. John Glenn is ready."[1]

The day was February 20, 1962. After weeks and months of delays, astronaut John Glenn was finally about to be launched into space. If the launch was successful, Glenn would become the first American to orbit Earth. Glenn sat in the cramped cockpit of his spacecraft, *Friendship 7*. His own teenage children, Carolyn and David, had given the craft its name.

As Glenn waited for launch, his friend and fellow astronaut Scott Carpenter took a call from Glenn's wife, Annie. He put it through to the spacecraft. Glenn spoke to Annie and their children.

He told them about the clouds he saw rolling by

above him. He cranked out his periscope and told them he could see the ground and the launchpad below him. He said he could feel the rocket swaying gently in the wind. He also could hear its metal skin snapping and pinging as the tanks were filled with super-cold liquid hydrogen fuel. Then he had to say good-bye to them. Maybe for the last time.[2]

No one had ever flown on top of an Atlas rocket. It had a history of failure. If it failed today, Glenn would probably be killed. Three years of training to go into space could end today in a fiery explosion. Or he could fly successfully into orbit, and so fly into history. This was a risk John Glenn was willing to take.

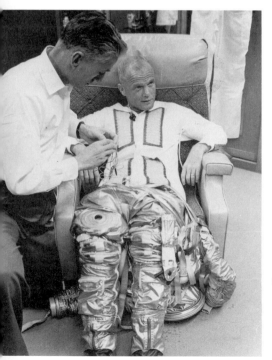

Millions of people around the world watched this drama unfold across their television screens. Bad weather and problems with the rocket had pushed the launch date back several times. The delays focused further attention on John Glenn and the dangerous challenge he was prepared to face.

Astronaut John Glenn wore a specially designed spacesuit for his flight.

John Glenn sat in the cramped cockpit of his spacecraft as he awaited the launch.

People learned much about Glenn from TV and the newspapers. He was almost a household name before ever going into space.

John Glenn grew up in New Concord, Ohio, and married his childhood sweetheart, Annie Castor. He was a Marine pilot in World War II and the Korean War. Glenn shot down three MiG fighter planes in nine days during his time in Korea. He also earned the name "Old Magnet Tail" for his habit of taking heavy enemy fire on his plane before pulling out over targets.

In 1957, Glenn gained national attention. He flew a F8U Crusader navy fighter across the United States and set the transcontinental jet speed record.

That was the same year the Soviets (the former Communist government of Russia) launched Sputnik, the first man-made satellite, into space. Two years later, Glenn became one of the seven Mercury astronauts who would pilot America's first manned space flights.

Two Americans had gone into space before Glenn. But a Soviet cosmonaut named Yuri Gagarin was the first person ever to go into space, on April 12, 1961. Gagarin had orbited Earth once. The American flights had not gone into orbit.

Weeks before Glenn's scheduled flight, another Soviet had orbited the Earth *sixteen times*. People in the United States, in western Europe, and other parts of the world were watching and hoping that Glenn's flight could match what the Soviets had done. In a few moments the waiting would be over.

"Looks good, old man," Scott Carpenter said from his station near the launchpad.

"Boy, can you imagine?" Glenn answered. "Here we go."

"Hot dog," Carpenter said.

John Glenn (left) chatted with fellow astronaut Scott Carpenter (right) before the launch.

Glenn listened to the voices in his headset. A final systems check signaled the countdown's final moments.

"Status check. Pressurization."

"Go."

"I have a blinking high-level light."

"You are go. Water Systems."

"Go."

"Range Operations."

"Go. Clear to launch."

"Mercury capsule."

"Go."

"All pre-start pilot lights are correct. The ready light is on. Eject Mercury umbilical. Oil evacuate."

"Mercury umbilical clear."

"Oil evacuate light is on."

"All recorders to fast. T minus eighteen seconds and counting. Engines start."

Two of the station communicators wished Glenn well.

Astronaut Scott Carpenter, a friend of John Glenn's, wished him luck before the flight.

"May the wayward winds be with you," said one.

"Good Lord ride all the way," said another.

From his friend Scott Carpenter came a final wish, and the countdown's last seconds. "God speed, John Glenn. Ten . . . Nine . . . Eight . . . Seven . . . Six . . . Five . . . Four . . . Three . . . Two . . . One . . . Zero."[3]

The rocket engines rumbled to life. A thick cloud of smoke mushroomed out to surround the launchpad. Bright orange flames gushed from beneath the Atlas rocket as it began to rise.

"Roger. The clock is operating. We're underway," Glenn said.[4] His voice was shaking as the rocket shook him on the bumpy ride.

Friendship 7 blasted off on the morning of February 20, 1962. Aboard was astronaut John Glenn.

Crowds along the beaches and roads surrounding Cape Canaveral, Florida, cheered as they watched Glenn's spacecraft thunder into the sky. They had waited a long time to see the launch. Now, the view of the rocket climbing higher and higher toward space was truly a thrilling sight.

John Glenn managed to keep himself calm during the exciting launch. But his adventure aboard *Friendship 7* was only beginning. Before it was over, the flight would challenge his skill as an astronaut, and greatly test his courage.

2

American in Orbit

Only two minutes after liftoff, *Friendship 7* was passing the speed of sound and rocketing faster and faster into space. John Glenn told Mercury Control the flight was "smoothing out real fine . . . flight very smooth now. Sky looking very dark outside."[1]

The G forces were building on Glenn's body as the rocket accelerated. His body was experiencing six Gs pressing down on him. This was six times his weight on Earth.

In a few moments the capsule would separate itself from the Atlas rocket and Glenn would be in orbit.

"Seven, Cape is Go. We're standing by for you," said Alan Shepard at Mercury Control. Shepard was also an astronaut. He had been the first American to go into space.

"Roger," Glenn said, "Cape is Go and I am Go. Capsule is in good shape." Suddenly he heard the explosive bolts separate the capsule from the rocket. He lurched forward slightly against his seat straps. Then he noticed that he floated there. The G forces were gone. He was weightless in space.

"Zero G and I feel fine," Glenn said. "Capsule is turning around." *Friendship 7* rolled over. Out his window, Glenn saw his first view of Earth from space. "Oh, that view is tremendous!"

Glenn also saw the Atlas rocket falling away below him. "The capsule is turning around and I can see the booster doing turnarounds just a couple of hundred yards behind me. It was beautiful."

"Roger, Seven," Shepard said. "You have a Go, at least seven orbits." Only three orbits were planned, but Shepard's comment confirmed *Friendship 7* had

John Glenn managed to keep himself calm during his exciting launch. His easy smile helped make him popular with the public.

achieved an orbit stable enough to make at least seven orbits.

"Roger. Understand Go for at least seven orbits. This is *Friendship 7.* Can see clear back, a big cloud pattern way back across towards the Cape. Beautiful sight."

The sight Glenn saw was from one hundred and twenty-five miles above the Earth. He was travelling through space at 17,500 miles per hour. After years of hard training, John Glenn was now the first American in orbit.

The view of Earth was a tremendous sight. But Glenn had a lot of work to do as he flew over the Atlantic Ocean toward Africa.

Friendship 7 was launched using an Atlas rocket such as the one diagrammed here. Note the spacecraft only takes up a small portion of the rocket's length.

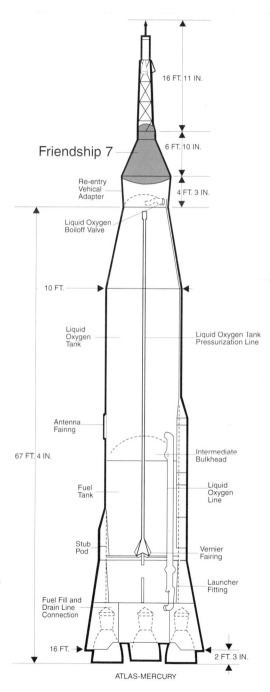

Friendship 7

16 FT. 11 IN.

6 FT. 10 IN.

Re-entry Vehical Adapter

4 FT. 3 IN.

Liquid Oxygen Boiloff Valve

10 FT.

Liquid Oxygen Tank

Liquid Oxygen Tank Pressurization Line

Antenna Fairing

67 FT. 4 IN.

Intermediate Bulkhead

Fuel Tank

Liquid Oxygen Line

Stub Pod

Vernier Fairing

Launcher Fitting

Fuel Fill and Drain Line Connection

16 FT.

2 FT. 3 IN.

ATLAS-MERCURY

John Glenn's view of the Atlantic Ocean as seen from space. He had a magnificent view of Earth below him.

Glenn tested the control thrusters, and made checks of many of the spacecraft's systems. He reported information about the capsule to tracking stations in Bermuda, the Canary Islands, and Zanzibar. He was the first American astronaut in orbit, so he told them about his sensations.

"This is very comfortable at zero G," Glenn said. "I have nothing but very fine feeling. It just feels very normal and very good."

Glenn saw large dust storms as he went over Africa. His orbit continued around to the dark side of Earth, into his first night orbital pass. He tried to describe his view of the sun setting below the Earth's horizon behind him.

"The sunset was beautiful. It went down very rapidly. I still have a brilliant blue band clear across the horizon. . . . The sky above is black, completely black. I can see stars though above. I do not have any of the constellations identified as yet. Over."

Glenn next came into range of the tracking station in Muchea, Australia. "That was about the shortest day I've ever run into," he told the capsule communicator (capcom). "Just to my right I can see a big pattern of lights apparently right on the coast. I can see the outline of a town and a very bright light just to the south of it."

The capcom told Glenn that these lights were coming from the Australian cities of Perth and Rockingham. The people in those cities had stayed up late into the night. They turned their lights on to be a night beacon to John Glenn flying over in space.

"Roger. The lights show up very well," Glenn said, "and thank everybody for turning them on, will you?"

Next, he tried to eat in space. He flipped up his helmet visor. Then he squeezed applesauce into his mouth from what looked like a toothpaste tube. No one knew what would happen if an astronaut ate in space. Glenn was supposed to try it. There were no problems.

Soon he saw the sun rising over the horizon ahead of him. Then something strange happened.

"This is *Friendship 7*, I'll try to describe what I'm in here." Glenn found his spacecraft surrounded by thousands of brightly shining particles floating in space. "I am in a big mass of some very small particles, that are brilliantly lit up like they're luminescent. I

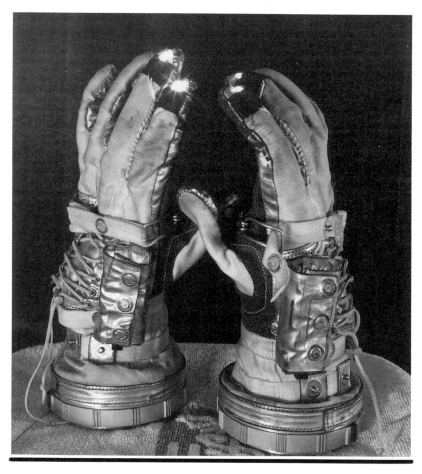

John Glenn wore these gloves during his flight. The lights on the glove's fingertips lit up when he orbitted the dark side of the Earth.

never saw anything like it . . . just at sunrise there are literally thousands of them. They look just like a myriad of stars." (On the next Mercury flight, astronaut Scott Carpenter learned that these particles were tiny ice crystals.[2] The crystals broke away from the side of the capsule as its metal skin warmed up in the sun.)

The flight had gone well, so far. Glenn was very busy checking instruments and doing brief experiments to test his adaptability to zero G. He was having a fun time.[3] This was an exciting time. He knew that he was an explorer. He was one of the first human beings to experience the sights and sensations of flying in orbit around Earth.

But before Glenn completed his first orbit, he and his spacecraft began to experience problems. John Glenn would have to use all his training and courage to face them.

3

Trouble in Space

Friendship 7's position in space was controlled by thrusters. These thrusters were equipped with an automatic control system. If one end of the capsule drifted to the right or left, or tipped up or down, the automatic controls would be activated. They would put the capsule back at the right attitude.

Glenn noticed that the front of the spacecraft kept drifting about twenty degrees to the right. The automatic controls kicked in and corrected for the drift. The drift was not a problem. The problem was that the automatic system was using a lot of thruster fuel to correct for the small error.

Glenn would need this fuel later to get *Friendship 7* into the proper position for reentering Earth's atmosphere. If he left the automatic control system on, it would continue to waste the thruster fuel. This might threaten Glenn's ability to maneuver the capsule into the proper angle for reentry. If he could not control the capsule's position during reentry, the capsule might burn up in Earth's atmosphere.

Glenn switched off the automatic system and took control of the spacecraft himself. He had to cancel some of the planned experiments, because he had to use all his attention to fly the spacecraft.

The thruster problem was not a big one. Glenn did a good job of conserving the thruster fuel for later in the flight. Glenn went into his second orbit. But now a new problem came up. This one was a serious threat to the mission, and maybe even John Glenn's life.

Mercury Control was getting a signal from the spacecraft that indicated that the landing bag was loose. The landing bag was coiled up like a jack-in-the-box behind the heatshield on the blunt end of the capsule. Its job was to soften the capsule's impact with the water as it drifted down by parachute to a splashdown in the Atlantic Ocean. The landing bag was programmed to pop out a few moments before the capsule landed.

The signal indicated that the landing bag had *already* popped loose. If it was loose, then the heatshield was loose too. And if the heatshield was loose, Glenn and *Friendship 7* would be burned to bits when they reentered Earth's atmosphere.

Mercury Control was not sure that the signal about the landing bag was correct. But they had to prepare for the worst. They did not tell Glenn about the signal for a while because he could not do anything about the landing bag if it was down. Mercury Control did not want to bother him with the news until just before reentry. They hoped that by that time they would either have solved the problem, or at least have a plan to deal with it.

Soon Glenn was flying over Australia again. During

Mercury Control back on Earth received a signal from the spacecraft that indicated the landing bag was loose.

the series of systems checks, the capcom in Australia asked, "Will you confirm that the landing bag switch is in the off position? Over."[1]

"That is affirmative," Glenn said, "landing bag switch is in the center off position."

Glenn flew into his second sunrise of the flight, but he did not have much time to enjoy the sight. He had switched off the automatic control system, but now the manual control system was giving him problems. When he moved the control stick, the thrusters moved the spacecraft too far in one direction, then not far enough in another. The thrusters were not responding accurately to his piloting commands.

Flying high over the Pacific Ocean, *Friendship 7* came in contact with the Canton Island station. The capcom on Canton Island thought Glenn had been told about the landing bag problem.

Glenn was puzzled when the capcom said, "We also have no indication that your landing bag might be deployed." This was the second time a capcom had mentioned the landing bag.

"Did someone report the landing bag could be down?" he asked.

The capcom said no. Mercury Control still did not want to tell him. Glenn flew over Hawaii and toward California. Mercury Control was deciding what to do about the landing bag and heatshield. They also needed to decide whether or not to have him do a third and final orbit.

As Glenn flew high above the Pacific Ocean, he communicated with the Canton Island capcom.

The signal said the heatshield was loose, but there was still hope that Glenn could return to Earth safely. A plan was beginning to take shape. On the blunt end of the spacecraft was something called the retro package. It was a set of three rocket thrusters that Glenn would fire to slow the capsule down. This loss of speed causes the capsule to fall from orbit and begin its long arc of reentry into the atmosphere.

The retro package was held onto the heatshield by three metal straps that were attached to the hull of the spacecraft. In a normal reentry, the retro package fires its rockets, then the straps detach and the retro package falls away. This leaves the heatshield bare and unobstructed to deal with the intense heat of reentry friction with Earth's atmosphere.

As long as the retro package straps stayed in place, they would hold the heatshield tightly against the hull of *Friendship 7*. Mercury Control decided to leave the straps in place during the entire reentry. This was the new plan. They hoped the straps would hold the heatshield in place long enough for the capsule to pass through the hottest part of reentry.

The capcom in Hawaii asked, "Do you still consider yourself go for the next orbit?"

"That is affirmative," Glenn said. "I am Go for the next orbit."

Friendship 7 continued into its third orbit around the world. Glenn had been facing backward for most of the flight. He was getting closer to the end of the mission, so he decided to use some thruster fuel to turn the capsule around. That way he could watch the sunrise ahead of him. Glenn had seen the other two sunrises from space through his periscope. He wanted to see this last one with his own eyes.

Now he had to prepare for the reentry sequence. He began stowing away any objects that were floating in the spacecraft. He also had to deal with another problem that had developed.

The gyroscopes were not giving him accurate readings about the capsule's attitude. Instead he had to look out the window and use the ground horizon as an attitude reference.

While he was orbiting in darkness over the Indian Ocean, Glenn had used the constellation Orion as a reference. He held the spacecraft's attitude by keeping the constellation centered in his cockpit window.

Glenn was now truly flying *Friendship 7* like a pilot flies a plane. He was changing the craft's attitude with hand controls and was using his eyes to keep it in proper position. He was the first astronaut from the United States or the Soviet Union to take this much control of a spacecraft in flight.[2]

Now he was flying over the Pacific toward Hawaii. He was about to learn that he might be flying himself and *Friendship 7* toward a fiery and tragic end.

4

Fireball in Space

The capcom in Hawaii had some potentially grave news for John Glenn.

"*Friendship 7,* we have been reading an indication on the ground of segment 51, which is Landing Bag Deploy. We suspect this is an erroneous signal. However, Cape would like you to check this by putting the landing bag switch in the auto position, and see if you get a light. Do you concur with this? Over."[1]

Now Glenn understood what all the landing bag talk had been about. But he wasn't thrilled with their recommendation. He did not want to play with the landing bag switch if they already suspected there was a problem with it.[2]

"Okay," Glenn said, "if that's what they recommend, we'll go ahead and try it. Are you ready for it now?"

"Yes," the capcom said, "when you're ready."

"Roger," Glenn answered. Without hesitation he reached forward and flipped the switch. "Negative, in automatic position did not get a light and I'm back in off position now. Over."

"Roger, that's fine. In that case we'll go ahead, and the reentry sequence will be normal."

As far as the Hawaii capcom knew, that was the plan. But it wasn't. The people at Mercury Control still did not think it was necessary to tell Glenn the plan for reentry. They believed he was very busy and did not need that information until later.

At the moment, Glenn was busy going through a checklist of all systems on the capsule before reentry. The thrusters and gyroscopes were still giving him problems as he maneuvered the capsule into position for retro fire.

The Hawaii capcom counted down toward retro fire, "Five . . . four . . . three . . . two . . . one . . . fire."

"Roger," Glenn said, "retros are firing . . . fire retro light is green." All three retro rockets fired perfectly. *Friendship 7* gradually began to fall from orbit. Glenn felt the sensation of normal gravity return.

"Keep your retro pack on until you pass Texas," the capcom told him.

"Roger," Glenn said, "Jettison retro is red. I'm holding onto it."

Because of the thruster problem, he had had trouble

holding the capsule in the correct position during retro fire. He could look forward to more of that during the reentry phase. The next message from Texas added to the difficult reentry he was about to make.

"This is Texas capcom, *Friendship 7*. We are recommending that you leave the retro package on through the entire reentry."

"This is *Friendship 7*. What is the reason for this? Do you have any reason? Over."

"Not at this time. This is the judgment of Cape Flight."

Glenn continued to prepare for reentry. A few minutes later he came into the range of Cape Canaveral and capcom Alan Shepard.

"Recommend you go to reentry attitude and retract the scope manually at this time," Shepard said.

"Roger, retracting scope manually," Glenn said.

"While you're doing that, we are not sure whether or not your landing bag has deployed. We feel it is possible to reenter with the retro package on. We see no difficulty at this time with that type of reentry. Over."

"Roger, understand," Glenn said calmly. He knew the spacecraft inside and out. He knew exactly why the controllers wanted him to keep the retro pack on.

However, the retro package was not a small piece of machinery. Glenn knew that when he reentered with it still attached to the heatshield he was going to have a very bumpy and fiery ride.

Soon Glenn heard a hissing sound. Occasionally orange flames flickered past his window. Reentry was starting. The capsule rocked and shook. It was a struggle to keep it at the proper reentry angle.

Then big orange-glowing chunks of something went past Glenn's window. His heartbeat began to quicken.

Glenn could not be sure what those orange chunks were. He hoped they were pieces of the retro package burning off. It was giving him a bumpy ride. He also knew it would burn off eventually. But what if it had already burned away? What if the heatshield was loose and the chunks he saw coming past his window were pieces of the landing bag and heatshield?

He heard a faint message from Mercury Control. He asked them to say it again. "Go ahead Cape. You're ground . . . you're going out," Glenn said.

"We recommend that you . . ." Communications were cut off. The intense heat of reentry created a barrier around the capsule that interrupted all communications.

Then Glenn saw a much bigger orange chunk go flying past his window.

"This is *Friendship 7,* I think the uh . . . pack just let go."

The spacecraft was streaking across the atmosphere like a flaming meteor. The friction with the atmosphere was slowing the capsule's speed and pressing Glenn into his seat with a force of about nine Gs.

At Mercury Control, astronaut Alan Shepard, capsule communicator, monitors the Friendship 7 reentry.

Strapped in the cockpit, Glenn struggled to keep the spacecraft at the proper angle with his hand controls. The flaming chunks flying past his window were now an inferno of flames.

"This is *Friendship 7,*" Glenn said. "A real fireball outside."

Mercury Control could not hear him. Because of the question about the heatshield, they were not certain they would hear from him again.[3] They simply had to wait for Glenn's voice to come through again after the reentry heat phase. Or not.

"*Friendship 7,* this is Cape. Do you read?" Shepard said repeatedly, waiting nervously for Glenn to reply. "*Friendship 7,* this is Cape. Do you read? Over."

Mercury Control kept waiting. There was only static on the radio. Again Shepard broadcast, "*Friendship 7,* this is Cape, do you read? Over." Suddenly there was a reply.

"Loud and clear. How me?" Glenn said.

"Roger, reading you loud and clear. How are you doing?"

"Oh, pretty good." It was all Glenn could think of to say after everything he had just been through.

Mercury Control gave him information about his position. He was going to land in the water only one mile from the recovery ships.

"What's your general condition?" Shepard asked. "Are you feeling pretty well?"

"My condition is good," Glenn said, "but that was a real fireball, boy. I had great chunks of that retro pack breaking off all the way through."

The parachutes then deployed from the capsule. "Main chute is on green," Glenn said with enthusiastic relief. "Chute is out in reef condition at 10,800 feet and . . . beautiful chute! Chute looks good! Rate of descent has gone to forty-two feet per second. The chute looks very good."

Friendship 7 splashed down safely in the Atlantic Ocean.

Nearly five hours after lifting off from Cape Canaveral, John Glenn and *Friendship 7* splashed down safely in the blue waters of the Atlantic. The heatshield had held. Glenn's flight as the first American to orbit Earth was a triumph.

Millions of Americans and people around the world had been watching. Now, America waited to greet this new hero as he returned from a historic voyage through space.

5

A Hero Returns

The U.S. Navy destroyer U.S.S. *Noa* hauled *Friendship 7* out of the water and placed it on the deck. Glenn was very hot inside his suit by now, and he was anxious to get out. He flipped a switch which blew open the hatch. Then he was helped out of the spacecraft.

As soon as he was standing on his feet, he was held still while someone painted a white outline around his first footprints on the deck. It was just the beginning of a hero's welcome unlike any other in American history.

There was a lot to celebrate.

The early 1960s were a time of tension between the United States and the former Soviet Union. The Soviets had been beating the United States in space accomplishments. But John Glenn's flight had restored

America's confidence in its space program. It made people believe that the United States could indeed compete in technical areas with the Soviet Union.

John Glenn's courage during this flight had made millions of Americans feel proud. When he returned from two days of debriefing about the flight, even

The crew of the recovery ship, the U.S.S. Noa, hauled the spacecraft out of the water and brought it on deck.

President John F. Kennedy greeted John Glenn back at Cape Canaveral. He awarded him a special medal.

President John F. Kennedy was there to meet him at Cape Canaveral. The wave of patriotism swept on from there.

Three days later, Glenn and his wife Annie went to Washington, D.C., to ride in a parade from the White House to the Capitol building. Because of his historic accomplishment, Glenn was given the honor of addressing a joint session of Congress.

"This has been a great experience for all of us on the program and for all Americans," Glenn said. "And I'm certainly glad to see that pride in our country and its accomplishments are not a thing of the past."[1]

Glenn tried to relate some sense of his experience in space. "The view from that altitude defies description. The horizon colors are brilliant and sunsets are spectacular," he said. "It is hard to beat a day in which you are permitted the luxury of seeing four sunsets."[2]

He described the tremendous organization and cooperation required for spaceflight. Then he closed his speech with a call to put what was learned from spaceflight to good purposes.

"We are all proud to have been privileged to be part

John Glenn addressed a joint session of Congress a few days after his historic flight.

of this effort, to represent our country as we have. As our knowledge of the universe in which we live increases, may God grant us the wisdom and guidance to use it wisely."[3]

John and Annie Glenn went to New York City three days later. Four million people lined the streets for a huge parade of celebration. The cheers from the crowd were deafening.

Their last parade was smaller but it was just as meaningful. John and Annie returned to their hometown of New Concord, Ohio. The town's population of 2,100 went up to 40,000 for the event.

John Glenn was honored when millions lined the streets in his honor at a New York ticker-tape parade. He rode with Vice President Lyndon Johnson.

John and Annie Glenn enjoyed riding in the New Concord, Ohio parade in their honor.

The flight of *Friendship 7* was the first U.S. manned orbital flight. It led the way for other orbital flights in the Mercury program—Scott Carpenter's flight in *Aurora 7,* Wally Schirra's flight in *Sigma 7,* and Gordon Cooper's flight in *Faith 7.*

These flights taught the U.S. space program many important things about spacecraft operation and human reaction to the space environment. The Mercury program paved the way for the Gemini program. This program would use a two-astronaut spacecraft. Astronauts in the Gemini program would practice the techniques of rendezvous and docking in

John Glenn was the hero of Friendship 7.

space. These techniques would be important for a trip to the Moon—the goal of the later Apollo program.

Friendship 7 and the Mercury program were the first steps toward a future in space for humanity. It often seems that the space program brings out some of the best of what human beings have to offer. It asks human beings to take on tremendous challenges and to overcome them with a special mix of intelligence, hard work, and dedication.

There was indeed something special about John Glenn.

At the time of the flight, an Associated Press reporter wrote that John Glenn "had made Americans feel better about being Americans. . . . In the saddle of success he rode loose and easy, and everyone found something to like."[4]

Astronaut John Glenn was the hero of the flight of *Friendship 7.*

CHAPTER NOTES

Chapter 1

1. Philip N. Pierce, *John H. Glenn, Astronaut* (New York: Franklin Watts, 1962), p. 1.

2. Peter N. Carroll, *Famous in America: The Passion to Succeed* (New York: Dutton, 1985), p. 70.

3. *To the Moon* (record documentary), Time/Life Records, 1970.

4. *Results of the First United States Manned Orbital Space Flight* (Washington, D.C.: National Aeronautics and Space Administration, 1962), p. 145. All in-flight communications that follow in this chapter come from this source.

Chapter 2

1. *Results of the First United States Manned Orbital Space Flight* (Washington, D.C.: National Aeronautics and Space Administration, 1962), p. 150. All in-flight communications that follow in this chapter come from this source.

2. *We Seven, By the Astronauts Themselves* (New York: Simon and Schuster, 1962), p. 457.

3. Ibid., p. 402.

Chapter 3

1. *Results of the First United States Manned Orbital Space Flight* (Washington, D.C.: National Aeronautics and Space Administration, 1962), p. 171. All in-flight communications that follow in this chapter come from this source.

2. Ibid., pp. 135–136.

Chapter 4

1. *Results of the First United States Manned Orbital Space Flight* (Washington, D.C.: National Aeronautics and Space Administration, 1962), p. 186. All in-flight communications that follow in this chapter come from this source.

2. Personal interview with John Glenn, June 18, 1991.

3. "Spaceflight Part 2: The Wings of Mercury," narrated by Martin Sheen, PBS Video (1985).

Chapter 5

1. Philip N. Pierce, *John H. Glenn, Astronaut* (New York: Franklin Watts, 1962), p. 179.

2. Ibid.

3. Ibid.

4. William R. Shelton, "America Finds A Hero," special report, in *1963 World Book Year Book* (New York: Field Enterprises Educational Corporation, 1963), p. 160.

GLOSSARY

Atlas rocket—A missile adapted by the U.S. space program for use as the booster rocket for the first manned orbital flights.

attitude—The position of an aircraft or spacecraft with reference to how its front, rear, or sides are tipped, turned, or rotated.

capcom (capsule communicator)—The person who communicates directly with the astronaut in the spacecraft; he is usually another astronaut.

control thrusters—Small rockets on the sides of the spacecraft that control its position in space.

G force—The force that is exerted on a body by gravity; also a measurement of how much additional force is being exerted on a body when it accelerates—a boy or girl who weighs 100 pounds in 1-G (normal Earth gravity) will weigh 200 pounds at 2-G acceleration.

gyroscope—Instrument used in aircraft and spacecraft to indicate the position or attitude of the craft.

heatshield—The surface on the blunt end of early spacecrafts. Parts of the surface were designed to burn away. This would carry the heat away and prevent heat from building up on the spacecraft.

jettison—To drop away or discard something.

landing bag—The coiled-up cushion packed into the blunt end of the Mercury spacecraft. It was designed to soften the spacecraft's impact with the water at splashdown.

periscope—A viewing instrument that uses mirrors to give a person a view that would otherwise be obstructed.

retro package—The rockets strapped to the blunt end of the Mercury spacecraft; these were fired to slow the spacecraft down to prepare for reentry.

FURTHER READING

Bond, Peter. *Heroes in Space: From Gagarin to Challenger*. New York: Basil Blackwell, Inc., 1987.

Cipriano, Anthony. *America's Journey Into Space*. New York: Julian Messner, 1979.

Cole, Michael D. *John Glenn: Astronaut and Senator*. Springfield, N.J.: Enslow Publishers, Inc., 1993.

Fenno, Richard F. *The Presidential Odyssey of John Glenn*. Washington, D.C.: Congressional Quarterly Press, 1990.

We Seven, By the Astronauts Themselves. New York: Simon and Schuster, 1962.

Wolfe, Tom. *The Right Stuff*. New York: Farrar, Straus & Giroux, 1979.

INDEX